# If You Were Me and Lived In...
# GERMANY

## A Child's Introduction to Culture Around the World

### Carole P. Roman
Illustrated by Kelsea Wierenga

# To Brigid and Agnieszka

# Danke schön

ISBN: 1539135942

ISBN 13: 978-1539135944

*Disclaimer:*

*Please note that there may be differences in dialect that will vary according to region. Multiple individuals*

*(from each country) were used as sources for the pronunciation key but you should be aware of the possibility*

*of alternative pronunciations.*

BERLIN

GERMANY

If you were me and lived in Germany (Ger-man-nee), you would call your country Deutschland (Doytch-lawnd), but the rest of the world would know it as the Federal Republic of Germany. You would find your home located in the northeastern part of Europe.

The word Germany comes from a Germanic word meaning folk or people.

Germany is a member of the European Union. The European Union is a group of countries on the European continent that chooses to make decisions together involving trade and money.

You would learn in school that Germany has sixteen states. It is the most populated member of the European Union and the second most popular immigration destination in the world.

You might live in the capital, Berlin (Ber-lin). Berlin is the largest city in Germany and located in the northeastern part of the country. It was built on the Rivers Spree (Spree) and Havel (Hav-el). One-third of the city's area is made up of forests, parks, gardens, rivers, and lakes.

Berlin has been an important city for centuries because it is located at the crossroads of two vital trade routes, bringing products from as far away as Italy to cities in Russia.

After World War II, Berlin was split by a huge wall, dividing it into two different countries. Families were separated. People weren't allowed to cross the wall to visit. In 1990, the wall came down, and Berlin was joined as one city again.

4

If you are a boy, your parents might have named you Lukas (Loo-kas), Johan (Yo-han), or Maximillian (Max-i-mil-yan). They may have named your sister Lena (Lee-na), Anna (An-na), or Emilia (Em-mil-ya).

Every day, Papa (Papa) would take you out to ride your Fahrrad (Fa-rhad) after he comes home from work. Your sister has one too but prefers to stay inside with Mama (Ma-ma) and play with her Puppe (Pu-peh). Can you guess what a Fahrrad and Puppe are?

Afterward, you would stop by Oma (O-ma) and Opa's (O-pa) house. You enjoy spending time with your grandparents. They might give you a Euro (Ur-roe) for Eistüte (Eyes-tut-ah). Opa would tell you that a Euro is not German money. It is a European currency that replaced the German marks that were used when he was a small boy.

When your Tante (Tan-ta) and Onkel (On-kul) come to visit, your sister always wants to take them to see Neuschwanstein (Noy-shwan-stein) Castle. Onkel is your mother's brother and Tante is his wife. She was born in America.

The castle is one of Europe's most beautiful and famous tourist sites. It can be seen high on a hill in the old town of Füssen (Fus-sen) in the Bavarian mountains. King Ludwig II built the castle during the years 1869-1886, and many say it was the inspiration for Walt Disney's famous castle in his Disneyland theme park. You love to visit the throne room and pretend you are the ruler of the country.

You tell your parents you would much prefer going to the historic Port Of Hamburg to visit the Miniatur Wunderland (Min-i-a-tur Vun-der-land). You enjoy seeing the world's largest model railway.

It has more than 800 trains, 300,000 lights, and over 200,000 figures of people playing out scenes in the United States, Hamburg, and Scandinavia. There are crowded cities, harbors, and farmland that look like the real thing! They have a model of an airport that has mini planes that take off.

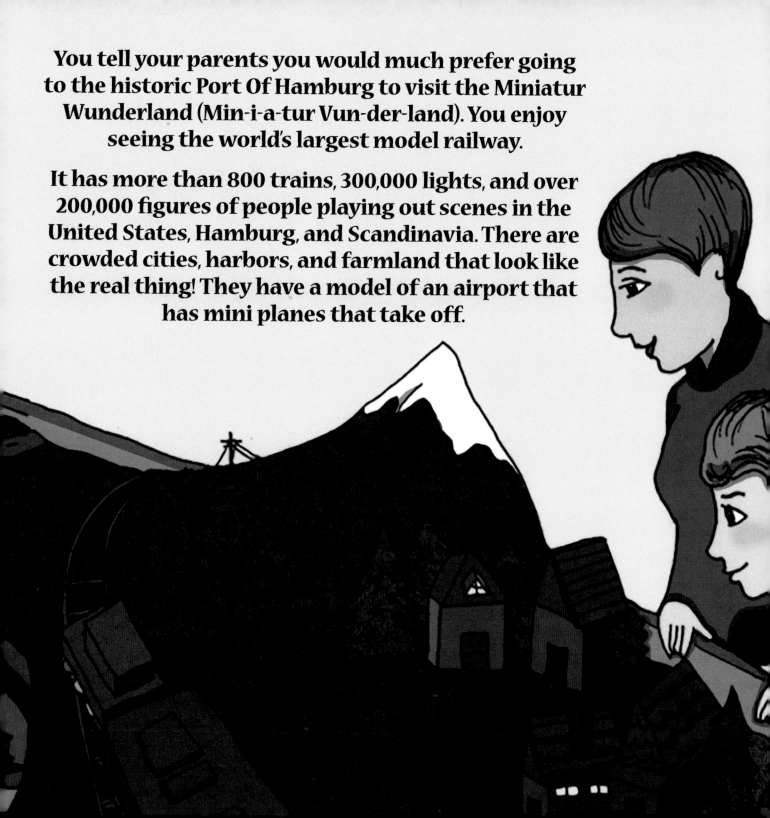

After all that walking, you would be hungry for a plate of Sauerbraten (Sa-wer-brat-ten). Beef or pork is marinated in vinegar and seasoning for up to ten days. The pot roast is then cooked and served with cabbage called Sauerkraut (Sa-wer-kraut) and dumplings or Knödel (K-new-del) made from potatoes.

Papa orders Wiener Schnitzel (Vee-ner Schnit-zel) which is a thinly pounded veal cutlet, coated in breadcrumbs, fried, and served with a slice of lemon. Onkel eats a Hamburg-style Schnitzel; it comes with a fried egg on top. Either way, the meal is finished with an Apfelstrudel (Ap-fel-stru-del). It is a buttery pastry filled with apples flavored with sugar, cinnamon, and raisins. The delicate, flaky pastry is made from an elastic dough, which is kneaded and stretched until it's almost paper thin. The thin pastry layers are buttered together before being wrapped around the apple filling and baked. It's served warm in slices sprinkled with powdered sugar. Yum.

You remind Papa you have to rush home to watch Fussball (Fuss-ball). Onkel has told you that when he visited the United States, he learned the Americans called it soccer.

Fussball is a very popular sport in Germany.  The German league called Bundesliga (Bund-es-lig-a) is one of the most famous and successful leagues in Europe. Every weekend, tens of thousands of fans support their favorite Fussball team and cheer for them.

Oncle comes from a small city in the countryside and doesn't have a Fussball team. He has invited both you and your father to see the exciting handball teams that play there.

In the fall, you will see Tante and Onkel at a great festival called Oktoberfest (Oct-to-ber-fest) that takes place in Munich (Mun-chen). You laugh when your American-born Tante mispronounces the Bavarian capital as *Mew-nick* and politely correct her.

It is a big fair with amusement rides, games, and attractions. You eat Wurst (Wur-st) or sausages until you are bursting.

Your sister loves the hot Brezel (Bre-zel). Mama makes you share the oversized pretzels. Papa munches on Aal (Aye-l) sandwiches. He enjoys the small pieces of eel cut up and eaten with bread. You are sure to find him Rollmops (Roll-mops) too. Marinated herring is rolled with a tasty pickle and stuffed in a bun as a filling snack.

If you sniff the air, you can smell the Schweinebraten (Schvein-a-braten) cooking. Roasted pork is your favorite treat.

The festival is over two hundred years old and a fun celebration of Bavarian culture.

You had to write a report on five important facts about Germany. Papa helped you find some interesting things.

1- The oldest sun observatory known in Europe is the Goseck (Go-sak) Circle in Saxony-Anhalt (Sax-on-ee- Ah-nalt). It was built about 7,000 years ago.

2- The Holy Roman Empire of the German Nation was founded by Charlemagne (Char-le-main) in 800 AD. It lasted over a thousand years.

3- Hildegard of Bingen (Hil-dee-gard of Bing-en) (1098-1179) was a composer. Her works are considered the foundation for what became known as opera.

4- One of the world's oldest savings bank was established in Oldenburg (Ol-den-burg) in 1786.

5- One of world's two biggest cuckoo clocks are both located in Baden-Württemberg (Bad-en Vurt-ten-berg). One of the cuckoos measures nearly 5 meters and weighs 150 kilograms or a little more than 16 feet and weighs more than 330 pounds. That's a big clock!

You plan to bring your information to Schule (Shoo-le).

Can you guess where that is?

So you see, if you were me, how life in Germany could really be.

# Glossary

Aal (Aye-l)- eel.

Anna (An-na)- a popular girl's name in Germany.

Apfelstrudel (Ap-fel-stru-del)- the flaky dough that has apples and sugar wrapped inside.

Bavarian (Ba-var-ee-an)- a state in southeastern Germany known for its beautiful castles and pretty villages.

Berlin (Ber-lin)- the capital of Germany.

Brezel (Bre-zel)- a pretzel.

cuckoo (koo-koo)- a medium sized long-tailed bird often used in clocks for its loud call to note the time.

currency (cur-ren-cee)- money.

danke schön (dots ver o) (Dan-kah schein)- thank you.

Disneyland (Dis-nee-land)- the famous American theme-park.

Deutschland (Doytch-lawnd)- the country called Germany in central and western Europe.

Eistüte (Eyes-tut-ah)- ice cream.

Emilia (Em-mel-ya)- a popular girl's name in Germany.

Euro (Ur-roe)- the currency used in the European Union.

Europe (Ur-rope)- the collection of countries in the European continent.

**European Union (Ur-pean Un-yun)**- a collection of countries that share the same currencies in Europe.

**Fahrrad (Fa-rhad)**- a bicycle.

**folk (fok)**- a collection of people with the same ethnic background or similar roots.

**Fussball (Fuss-ball)**- soccer.

**Füssen (Fus-sen)**- a Bavarian town in Germany.

**Gemanic (Ger-man-ik)**- having characteristics stemming from German people or Germany.

**German marks (Ger-man marks)**- old German money.

**Germany (Ger-man-nee)**- a country in central and western Europe.

**Hamburg (Ham-burg)**- a major port city in Germany.

**Havel River (Ha-vel)**- a river in the northeastern part of Germany.

**immigration (im-mi-gra-ti-shun)**- moving from one country to live in another.

**Italy (It-tal-lee)**- a country in southern Europe.

**Johan (Yo-han)**- a popular boy's name in Germany.

**King Ludwig II (Lud-wig)**- King of Bavaria in the 1800s.

**Knödel (K-new-del)**- dumplings made from potato.

**league (leeg)**- a group of sports clubs.

**Lena (Le-na)**- a popular girl's name in Germany.

**Lukas (Loo-kas)**- a popular boy's name in Germany.

**Mama (Ma-ma)**- Mommy.

**marinated (ma-ra-nade)**- soaking food in spices to make them taste good.

**Maximillian (Max-i-mil-yan)**- a popular boy's name in Germany.

**Miniatur Wunderland (Min-i-a- tur- Wun-der-land)**- a miniature model railway in Hamburg, Germany.

**Munich (Mun-chen)**- capital of Bavaria region of Germany. Pronounced Mew-nick by non-Germans.

**Neuschwanstein (Noy-shwan-stein) Castle**- the Bavarian castle built in the 1800s. It was the model for Disneyland's famous Cinderella castle.

**observatory (ob-serv-it-tor-ee)**- a building with a large telescope to look at the stars.

**Oktoberfest (Oct-to-ber-fest)**- a huge German festival with games, music, dancing, and plenty of food.

**Onkel (On-kul)**- an uncle.

**Oma**- Grandma.

**Opa**- Grandpa.

**Papa (Pa-pa)**- Daddy.

**Puppe (Pu-peh)**- a doll.

**Rollmops (Roll-mops)**- marinated herring rolled with a pickle and eaten with bread.

Russia (Rus-sha)- a large country in eastern Europe.

Sauerbraten (Sa-wer-brat-ten)- German pot roast.

Sauerkraut (Sa-wer-kraut)- pickled cabbage.

Scandinavia (Scan-da-nav-ee-ya)- the country in northwestern Europe.

Schule (Shoo-le)- a school.

Schweinebraten (Schai-na-bra-ten)- pork roast.

Spree River (Spree)- a river that flows through Germany.

Tante (Tan-ta)- an aunt.

throne (thron)- a seat where a king sits and holds court.

vinegar (vin-a-gar)- a liquid used to pickle foods.

Wurst (Wur-st)- sausage.

Wiener Schnitzel (Ween-ner Schnit-zel)- breaded veal cutlet.

Made in the USA
Columbia, SC
12 January 2021